# How to Get that Job

## Ace the Interview and Get Hired today

Introduction

I want to thank you and congratulate you for downloading the book, "How To Get That Job: Ace The Interview and Get Hired Today." This book contains proven steps and strategies on how to handle high impact and high powered job interviews.

This book will provide a systematic approach on how to tackle job interviews effectively and successfully get the job that you want. This systemic approach will give readers a 360 degrees approach on the interview process and pinpoint very important factors in order to handle job interviews like a professional. Whether you are a first time job hunter or still looking for that big opportunity, this ebook will help you get hired today.

The objective of this book is not to tell you what went wrong but rather to add more weapons to your arsenal for when you next "go into job interview battle". It is also for making sure that you are fully equipped for your first time job interview.

Thanks again for downloading this book, I hope you enjoy it!

© **Copyright 2014 by Anthony Worthington - All rights reserved.**

This document is geared towards providing exact and reliable information in regards to the topic and issue covered. The publication is sold with the idea that the publisher is not required to render accounting, officially permitted, or otherwise, qualified services. If advice is necessary, legal or professional, a practiced individual in the profession should be ordered.

- From a Declaration of Principles which was accepted and approved equally by a Committee of the American Bar Association and a Committee of Publishers and Associations.

In no way is it legal to reproduce, duplicate, or transmit any part of this document in either electronic means or in printed format. Recording of this publication is strictly prohibited and any storage of this document is not allowed unless with written permission from the publisher. All rights reserved.

The information provided herein is stated to be truthful and consistent, in that any liability, in terms of inattention or otherwise, by any usage or abuse of any policies, processes, or directions contained within is the solitary and utter responsibility of the recipient reader. Under no circumstances will any legal responsibility or blame be held against the publisher for any reparation, damages, or monetary loss due to the information herein, either directly or indirectly.

Respective authors own all copyrights not held by the publisher.

The information herein is offered for informational purposes solely, and is universal as so. The presentation of the information is without contract or any type of guarantee assurance.

The trademarks that are used are without any consent, and the publication of the trademark is without permission or backing by the trademark owner. All trademarks and brands within this book are for clarifying purposes only and are the owned by the owners themselves, not affiliated with this document.

# Chapter 1: Elements of a High Powered Job Interview

A job interview is the most important aspect in the selection process. For the employers, it is their means to search for the most suitable applicants to be a part of their companies. And for the applicants, it is their chance to present to their future employers and showcase what they can offer for them.

Thus, when you are called for a job interview, this is now the chance for you to tell companies why you are the right person for the job. Before you show yourself for a job interview, it is important to know the rigors in order for you to be hired right away.

It is right to consider it as one of the most important appointments that you will encounter in your entire life. The outcome of this process has a great impact on a career whether if it is your first interview or you have already made a career out of job interviews.

There are four elements in the job interview process that you have to consider:

- Preparation for the interview – what you should do before the formal interview process.
- Verbal Aspects of the job interview – what are involved on top of words and sentences.

- Non-Verbal Aspects of the interview – how body language affect your chance of being hired right away.

- Formulation of Winning Answers – what questions to anticipate and how you should give responses.

These elements will help you focus on what to do before, during, and after the interview in order to get that job. Each of these elements will be discussed individually in the succeeding chapters.

# Chapter 2: Preparing For A Job Interview

Employment counselors would recommend that once an employer decides to call an applicant for an interview, the applicant should immediately schedule the interview and confirm it. Once this aspect is done, the applicant should make some preparations prior to the scheduled interview. There are two kinds of preparation job hunters must do prior to a scheduled job interview: basic and initiatives

Basic Preparation

These are the usual preparation discussed in many books, suggested by employment counselors, and recommended by employers themselves:

1. Know your future employer – it is surprising to know that there are still would be employees who present themselves for a job interview with little knowledge about their future employers. A little knowledge, at the least, about the company will boost your chances of employment as employers will see this that you are serious to work with them.

And, it is no excuse that right now that you do not have access to information, as the internet is one huge free library; a visit to the company website and a click on the "about us" button will only take 30 minutes at the most to learn about your future company or employer.

2. Find out more about the job you are applying for or the job that you want to have – it is a big "no no" to say that you are applying for any available position.  If the job ad stated the specific position, find out additional details on what the position is all about.  If you are applying randomly, be sure that you know what kind of job you are willing to accept and that you can do it confidently.  Knowing more details about the job can give you insights as to if you are suited with the job and can defend yourself when asked during the interview why are you are the most qualified for the job.

3. Find out logistics for the interview – it is not enough that you are properly

dressed for the occasion. It is also vital that you are dressed appropriately. For example, the company that you are applying might have certain bias against colors and dress styles.

Find out how to reach their office and do not forget to include in the preparation all modes of transportation. You need to know all routes should there be situations like heavy traffic.

4. Organize documents to bring – all your important papers and files should be placed inside a folder or an envelope and should be properly labeled so that you will not have

difficulty pulling it out when you need them.

5. Formulate your questions - job interview is two-way traffic. It is your chance to be clarified if you have questions lingering in your mind. Asking the right questions will show employers that you are indeed serious with your job application and it is not a random selection process on your part.

Initiative Preparation – refers to any pre-job interview preparation that is important and relevant but not usually covered by the usual job interview preparations. Some of these might be:

1. Find out more about the community the company office is located – this

information will give you ideas on formulating winning answers (this will be discussed in another chapter.) In addition, it will help you understand more about the company.

2. Find out more (if possible) on the people who will interview you. A lot of future employees have this notion that people from Human Resource will do the interview and they are quite wrong as not all companies rely on this department to do job interviews for them. For example, if you happen to know that one of the owners will be joining the panel interview, you will really prepare for the interview more than you can think of. Or, if you happen to have first hand information that one of the

interviewers is a stickler for first impressions, then you should know what to do to gain his or her impression.

3. Find out more on the corporate culture and the set of behaviors that it accepts. While you are not expected to follow their culture and norms, it is a plus factor if you are aware with it. If you find some of these quite different from what you practice and believe then the right way is to educate and familiarize yourself. Knowing the unwritten rules might help foster your cause so that you could be hired immediately. If you think you cannot stomach what you discovered then why wait for this interview in the first place.

# Chapter 3: Verbal Aspects of a Job Interview

A job interview is not all about the words that you use as part of your winning answers. You might look pleasant and your resume looks good on paper but you have also have to sound good during the interview. There are several factors to consider on the verbal aspect of job interviews

1. Pacing of your verbal responses – correct pacing means the right speed of delivering your words. A job interview is a conversation and you should deliver your sentences in a manner as if you are having a conversation with familiar people.

2. Pronunciation - you must be clear with your words when speaking; avoid mumbling and stuttering, these are not hallmarks of possible employees for any type of business.

3. Vocal variety – being in conversation with an interviewer doesn't mean that you have to be monotonous. Change the tone of your voice, if there is a need to make a strong voice to emphasize a point, so be it. If there is a need to tone down your voice to gain empathy from the interviewers, do so.

4. Enthusiastic tone – you must be energetic and passionate when giving answers. Eagerness and excitement must be evident when you respond and your tone must show that you are

well motivated and dynamic. Do not try to be humorous if you cannot pull it off.

5. Voice projection – you must maintain a comfortable vocal projection; not too loud or not too soft. Your voice should be pleasant to the interviewer and it should complement their voice projection also. Do not make the mistake of being loud mouthed during the interview process.

6. The message is the medium and the medium is the message. This old adage simply means that you really have to get your message across. While grammar and syntax and pronunciation are important, it is more

important that you can express clearly what you want to relay.

As an example, there are people who can command sentences that are heavy on words but do not mean anything at all.

It takes a lot of practice to incorporate all these verbal aspects. For a start, you can try practicing by reading news items, orating in the shower, or speaking to yourself while driving. It also helps to have someone to give you objective feedback with regard to these aspects of communication.

Another thing to remember is that, you are subjecting yourself for a job interview thus, before you worry about grammar and syntax, think first if you have gotten your message across your audience.

## Chapter 4: Non - Verbal Aspects of a Job Interview

If you think that verbal aspects will help you win the coveted job, then, you got it all wrong. Non-verbal aspects or body language in job interview includes facial expressions, gestures, and postures. These actions are either manifested consciously or unintentionally. The problem in this aspect is that countless articles were written on this area but still violations are accumulating when it comes to non-verbal signals. Here are body signals that you should watch out for during the interview process.

1. Make eye contact to the interviewer so that you will be perceived as confident and very clear with your intention to

work with the company. Eye contact helps build rapport with the interviewer. One thing to remember is that staring is different from reasonable eye contact.

2. Maintain good posture by sitting up straight and not slouching in your chair. A good posture shows that you have a commanding presence and are a very confident person. In some cases, future employers gauge good posture as a sign of being trustworthy. Do not forget that our real feelings are shown through our posture.

3. Avoid mannerisms that distracts interviewers such as shaking your legs, fidgeting, knuckling your fingers, rubbing your pants with your palms,

frequent clearing of throat, and other signs of being nervous or lacking in confidence. Not only these mannerisms are can distract your interviewers, it will make you look awkward and feel uncomfortable. Thus, your chance of getting hired will become dimmer because of these distractive mannerisms. In many cases, body language contradicts what we express in words.

4. Appear neat and well kept. The way you carry yourself helps provide a better impression on your part. Do not appear in a job interview with wrinkled clothes, with bad body odor, with ruffled hair, and other signs of poor hygiene. You do not want to ruin your chances with being untidy and smelly.

5. Do not forget to smile always. It is an indication that you have a positive attitude. A smile can help to relax both the interviewer and interviewee.

6. Maintain a reasonable space during interview. It is not proper to be very comfortable while in front of the interviewer. Some of the common mistakes and often ignored are:

   a. Leaning the body towards the interviewer.

   b. Picking things on the table.

   c. Going head to head while raising important ideas.

   d. Using hand gestures that extends near the body of the interviewer.

To prepare yourself with non-verbal aspects of job interview, you can practice by observation. Look around and guess what interactions are involve when you look at people beside you or near you. Test yourself use these different body languages to other people and take note of their reactions.

Future employers or interviewers are very sensitive with non-verbal aspects as it helps them provide additional information to solidify their instincts and hunches and become more objective with the selection process.

## Chapter 5: Formulating Winning Answers

Now that you have learned about preparing for job interviews and the verbal and non-verbal aspects of the process, it is now time for you to be well informed on the most critical element in job interview system process; giving winning answers. Accordingly, the best preparation is anticipating possible questions, formulating appropriate answers, and of course practicing.

Before everything else, you must bear in mind that:

1. You cannot predict the questions that will be asked during the interview. Thus, it is wise to expect the unexpected.

2. All sample answers that you find online or gathered around should be treated as guides exclusively. The interviewer can detect right away if your answers are scripted or not.

3. You should not be afraid with questions instead, you should treat these questions as opportunities to present yourself as the best candidate for the job. The important factor here is that your responses should be construed as the better answers from the rest of the applicants.

Here are the things that you should do before going over the question and answer preparation phase for your job interview:

1. Make an inventory of your skills, experiences, qualifications, personal backgrounds, traits, and characteristics that you think are relevant to the position that you are applying with.

2. Go over a sample list of interview questions that you gathered from various sources and at the same time create your own set of possible questions (these possible questions are dependent on the inventory that you made in item number 1.) For example, if you are asked what your strengths are do not assume that the next question will be all about your weaknesses. What if the interviewer tells you that one of your strengths is

a possible weakness in their company?

3. Review your answers, not just twice but multiple times, until you find it that your responses are just quite right. As a word of advice, do not attempt to memorize them, instead, remember the important ideas that you want your responses to convey.

4. Remember that stories sell. When you responding to important job interview questions such as "have you ever dealt with an aggressive person?" A good response would be "it was quite often while I was working in the complaint department of a utility company, I do remember different types of aggression I

encountered and so on and so forth." In other words, you should be able to convey an interesting and unique anecdote.

5. Do not forget the "You" point of view. You might think that this one is limited to writing business letters but nope it isn't. You must put yourself in the shoes of the interviewer. Thus, before formulating your answer, you should ask, what does the interviewer wants to hear? The answer, most times, is that interviewers want to hear accomplishments.

6. Do not ignore what you wrote in your resume. Most of the initial questions that will be asked are based on the

content that you presented in these documents.

You might want to formulate answers on these popular job interview questions for a start:

1. What are your strengths and weaknesses?
2. Why do you want to work with our company?
3. How do you see yourself in 5 years from now?
4. Why did you leave or why do you want to leave your company at this moment?
5. What accomplishments that you are proud of or what have you done that you want to forget?

6. How did you know about this vacancy?
7. Discuss your resume in 5 sentences?
8. How much salary do you expect?
9. Why we should hire you now?
10. Do you have any regrets or failure at this point in time?
11. How do you handle stress and pressure?
12. What excites you?
13. How do you best describe yourself; a follower or a leader?
14. Do have any hobbies?
15. What are the things that you are so uncomfortable with?

In order for your preparation on this element not to go to waste, here are some suggested actions that you can do so that you will be very comfortable in your job interview.

1. Role playing – this will help you acclimatize with the interview process.
2. Mind setting – it is all about picturing in your mind possible question and answer moment that will happen with your job interview.
3. Note taking – list down all possible questions and appropriate responses. Review from time to time and it will help if you have someone who can help you determine if the response is appropriate or not.

4. Audio recording – you can play it again and again and at the same time you can review your responses if it still relevant or not.

5. Video recording – this will help you identify the non-verbal aspects that are detrimental during job interview.

## Chapter 6: Conclusion

In summary, a systemic approach to a job interview is all about identifying the different kind of skills that you need in the interview process in order to get the job right away. You need to work on these skills:

1. Preparing for an interview.

2. Handling the verbal aspects of the interview.

3. Managing the non-verbal aspects of the interview.

4. Formulating winning answers for the interview.

In addition, the elements discussed in different chapters provided you with the following important ideas that you should always bear in mind in order to get the job right now:

1. The interviewer is not the executioner but rather as a director who will guide you to reveal important aspects about your life personally and professionally.

2. It is a two way communication process where the employer does not only have the right to ask questions but the future employees as well. A communication process where the obvious and the intrinsic are of equal importance yet, companies will not proclaim that the reason they hired is due to the non-verbal signals that you made.

3. Practice makes perfect. Thus, do not be disappointed if you will not get the job right, especially if it is your first time to experience a job interview.

4. Leverage is not exclusive to employers. As future employees, job interview is a means to show to companies what you can do and what they cannot give.

Thank you again for downloading this book!

I hope this book was able to help you to get your dream job, or help a friend realize his dream, or a relative trying to land a job. Job interviews can be tricky. As discussed in this book, you should not be afraid but instead, treat it as your own method to advertise yourself why you are the right person for the job.

The next step is to review your job interview experiences and tune up some of your responses based on the elements presented in this ebook. Learning is an ongoing process, even if you have a job right now, it does not mean that you have to be relaxed and believed that you will not need all of the above ideas.

Finally, if you enjoyed this book, then I'd like to ask you for a favor, would you be kind enough to leave a review for this book on Amazon? It'd be greatly appreciated!

Thank you and good luck!

www.ingramcontent.com/pod-product-compliance
Lightning Source LLC
Chambersburg PA
CBHW051825170526
45167CB00005B/2167